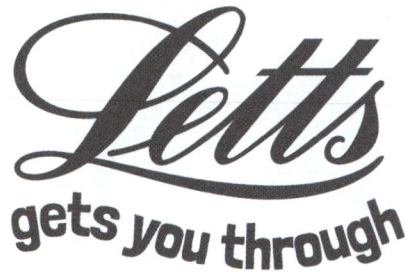

POETRY
PRACTICE WORKBOOK
WITH ASSESSMENT TESTS

Ages 10–11

11+ POETRY

FOR INDEPENDENT SCHOOL ENTRANCE

PRACTICE WORKBOOK WITH ASSESSMENT TESTS

11+

LOUISE LANG

Contents

About This Book — 3

Section 1: Understanding a Poem

'Books' by Lindsay Staniforth
First Reading — 4
Activity 1 — 4
Example Summary — 5
Second and Successive Readings — 6
Annotation — 7
Activity 2 — 8
Answering Questions on a Poem — 8
Example Questions and Answers — 10
Activity 3 — 11

'The Listeners' by Walter de la Mare
First Reading — 12
Activity 4 — 13
Example Summary — 13
Second and Successive Readings — 14
Example Questions and Answers — 15
Activity 5 — 16

Section 2: Assessment

Test 1 — 18
Test 2 — 20
Test 3 — 22
Test 4 — 24
Test 5 — 26
Test 6 — 28
Test 7 — 30
Test 8 — 32

Section 3: Example Answers and Guidance

Example Answers and Guidance — 34
Glossary of Key Terms — 55

About This Book

Poetry in Entrance Exams
As part of the comprehension section of English papers in 11+ independent schools entrance exams, your child will be given a factual or fictional passage to read and answer questions on. The texts are selected by the setters without any standard pattern and may well include a poem.

For any child, tackling a poem they have not seen before can be intimidating. This book gives them the opportunity to analyse a variety of different poems and to answer exam-style questions on them, so that they can respond to any poems that appear in the exam with confidence.

How to Use This Book
Section 1 of this book will guide your child through the process of reading and re-reading a poem to gain a good understanding of what it is about and develop a personal response. It includes example questions and answers with helpful tips. It will provide your child with a good framework to use whenever they are given a poem to analyse.

Section 2 comprises eight tests based on a variety of different poems, so that your child can practise analysing unseen poems.

Each test includes a number of exam-style questions. To help your child prepare for the exam, the questions may be completed under timed conditions. Allow 30 minutes for each test.

Following on from each test, there is a 'Challenge Question'. This is a higher level question that, in most cases, requires a carefully considered personal response. No example answers are given for these extension activities as there are an unlimited number of possible responses. The purpose of these activities is to encourage your child to really think about the poems in depth and guidance is given to get them started. Discuss your child's responses with them to help them explore and explain their ideas further.

Section 3 includes an example answer for each question, plus guidance on how to approach the question / what the examiner is looking for.

A glossary of key terms is included at the back of the book. The first time a key term is used within the book, it appears in blue. Some terms are not used within the book but have been included in the glossary for reference. It is a good idea for your child to learn these terms and then to revise them before the exam. Help your child to understand more difficult terms by discussing their meaning and then encouraging them to look for examples in different poems.

Supporting Your Child
The best way to help prepare your child for the comprehension section of 11+ English entrance exams is to foster a love of reading.

Introduce your child to lots of different types of text, including fiction, non-fiction and poetry. Try to avoid making reading a chore by finding texts that interest and engage your child. Talk to them about what the text is about and how it makes them feel. If you have a different response to a text, listen to what your child thinks first and then share your thoughts.

Encourage your child to use a dictionary to look up the meanings of unfamiliar words. Writing them in a notebook to create their own personal dictionary can be a beneficial and useful activity to help build vocabulary.

'Books' by Lindsay Staniforth

First Reading

When reading a poem, first you need to try to understand what it is about.
Most poems will require more than one reading to do this.

Try this one…

Books

There is something that is portable, renewable and cheap;
You can use it when you wake up or before you go to sleep; 2
It can make you weep with laughter; it can teach you how to cook;
It can take you to the future or the past. It's called a book. 4

If you want to know what life's like in a country far away,
Or you'd like to know what happened back in Charles the Second's day; 6
If you yearn to know what motivates the martyr or the crook
You will find these things and more between the covers of a book. 8

If you're a girl and want to know the inner thoughts of men,
Or a chap to whom a woman's mind is far beyond your ken, 10
You can enter other people's heads – you only have to look
At ink on paper – all the words that go to make a book. 12

by Lindsay Staniforth (1951–)

What is the poem about? Do you need to read it again? If so, go ahead.
Read it as many times as you need.

Activity 1

Write a short summary of what the poem is about.

Think about these questions:
- **What** is happening?
- **Who** is it happening to?
- **Why** is it happening?
- **How** is it happening?

Helpful Tip...
Not all poems are about something 'happening', but you still need to think about **what**, **who**, **why** and **how**, e.g.
- **What** is the poem about?
- **Who** is the poet addressing?
- **Why** is the poet writing this?
- **How** does the poet get their message across?

Example Summary

Here is an example summary. Compare it to your own.

What is happening / what is the poem about?
This poem is about the joy of books and what they can teach us. The poet is telling us about the good things that reading a book can bring.

Who is it happening to / who is the poet addressing?
The poet is addressing the reader, i.e. talking to us – 'you can use it' if you're 'a girl' or 'a chap'. She describes people and situations, providing us with examples of what and how we can learn through reading.

Why is it happening / why is the poet writing this?
The poet is telling us about the positive things that books can do for us and how they aid our learning. There is a sense that this is a celebration of books and the poet sees them as a positive influence in life.

How is it happening / how does the poet get their message across?
The poet guides and teaches us by providing examples. We can learn about different countries, 'far away'; about history, 'back in Charles the Second's day'; and about people, 'what motivates the martyr or the crook.' We can 'enter other people's heads' and learn about their 'inner thoughts'. She finishes by telling us that all of this information and experience is easy for us to access: we 'only have to look | At ink on paper' and read 'all the words that go to make a book'.

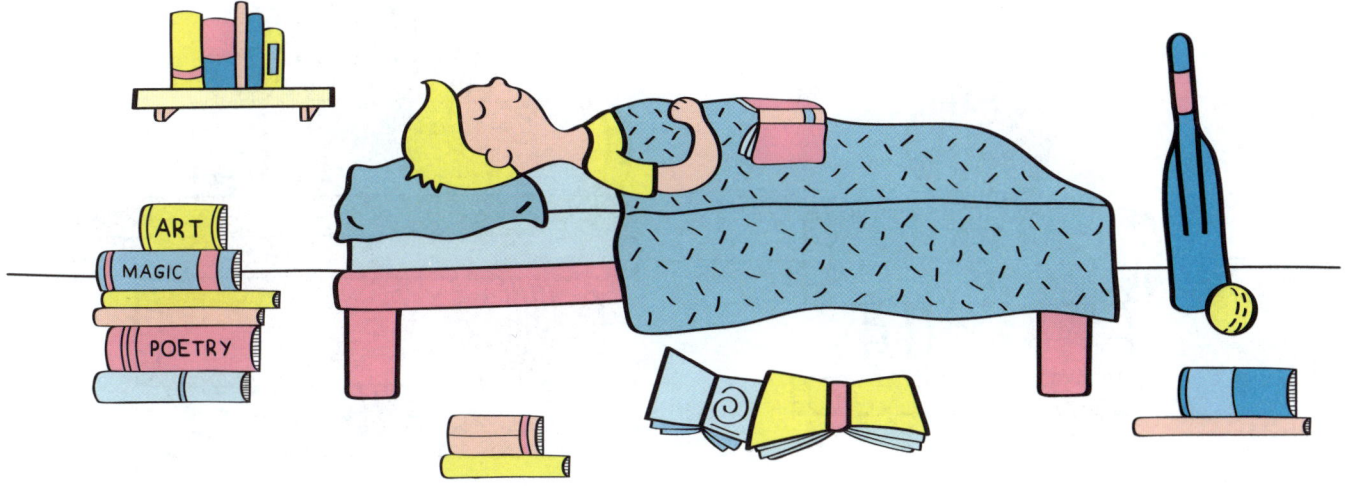

Second and Successive Readings

As you read the poem again, keep thinking about **what**, **who**, **why** and **how**. Also ask yourself, 'what **feelings** can I sense?'

All poetry is about **emotion** and feelings:
- How does the poet or **narrator** feel?
- How do the characters or **protagonists** in the poem feel?
- How do you, the reader, feel?

As you re-read and begin to understand a poem more, start to look out for any patterns, **contrasts** (differences) and **themes** that appear throughout the poem. For example, the poem 'Books' includes:

Patterns:
- three **stanzas** (verses) of four lines each
- rhyming words at the end of each pair of lines (rhyming couplets)
- **repetition** of 'you' as the poet talks to the reader
- repetition of the phrases 'it can' and 'if'.

Contrasts:
- contrast of ideas, e.g. 'when you wake up or before you go to sleep'
- contrast of words / images, e.g. 'weep with laughter', 'future or the past'
- the poet is addressing both male and female readers, e.g. 'If you're a girl… | Or a chap'.

Themes:
- learning and knowledge
- access to knowledge
- universality
- timelessness.

Every poem has themes. Some will be very obvious, others less so. Responses to themes in a poem are often a personal thing. Whilst you should always address the obvious ones, you may identify lesser ones that are meaningful to you but may not be apparent to somebody else.

Annotation

Make notes next to the poem. This is called **annotation**. Always link a note to a specific word or phrase, so you know what it refers to. This saves time later when you have to answer questions on the poem and need to find specific examples to back up what you are saying about it.

This may seem like a long process, but it will pay off in the end!

Here is an example of annotations identifying some of the points made about 'Books'.

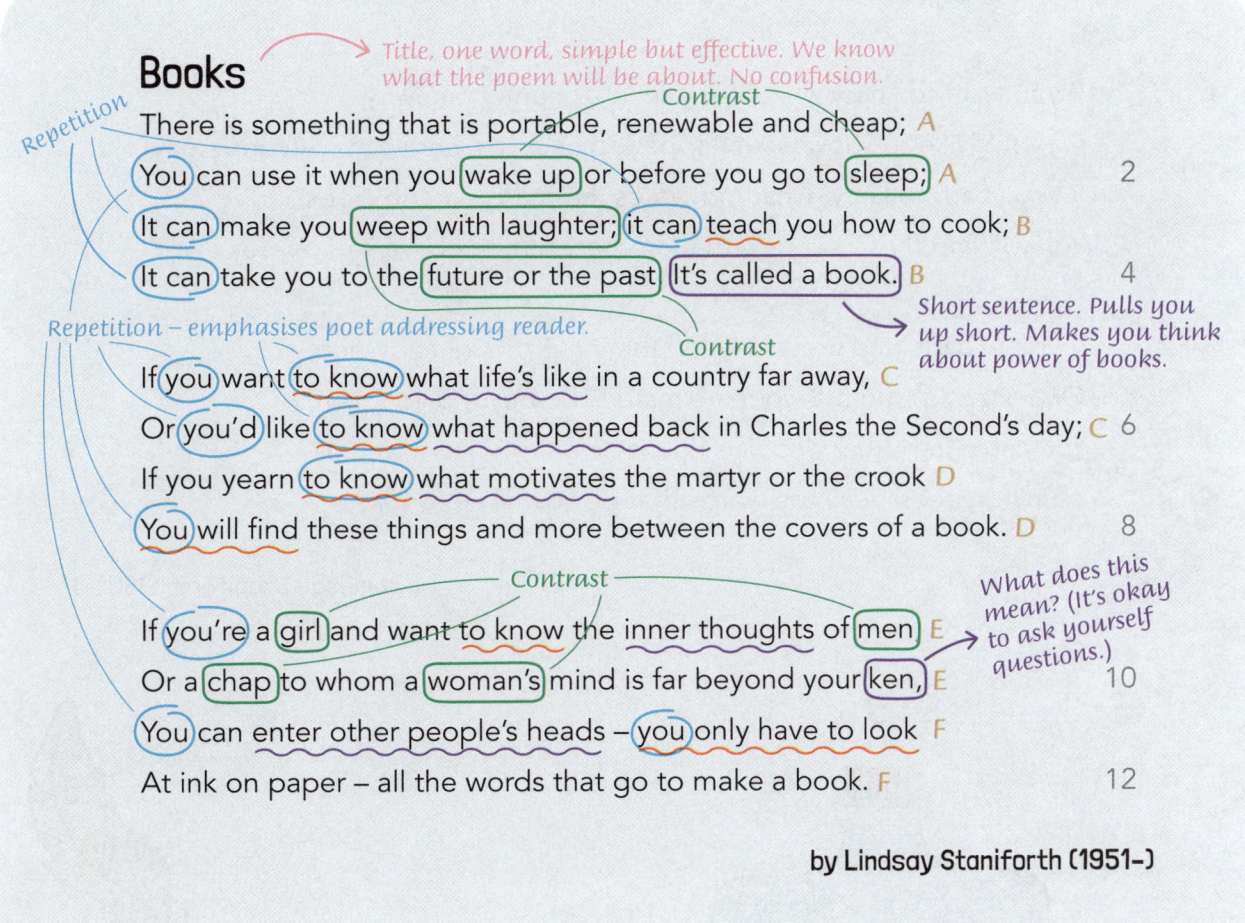

Key

A–F   Rhyme scheme

~~~~ Theme of teaching / learning / education

~~~~ Theme of what you can learn from books / how exciting they are / positive influence of books.

*Annotate as you **want** – make the poem yours!*

Activity 2

Here is another copy of 'Books'. Annotate and add your own ideas to the poem.

Books

There is something that is portable, renewable and cheap;
You can use it when you wake up or before you go to sleep;   2
It can make you weep with laughter; it can teach you how to cook;
It can take you to the future or the past. It's called a book.   4

If you want to know what life's like in a country far away,
Or you'd like to know what happened back in Charles the Second's day;   6
If you yearn to know what motivates the martyr or the crook
You will find these things and more between the covers of a book.   8

If you're a girl and want to know the inner thoughts of men,
Or a chap to whom a woman's mind is far beyond your ken,   10
You can enter other people's heads – you only have to look
At ink on paper – all the words that go to make a book.   12

by Lindsay Staniforth (1951–)

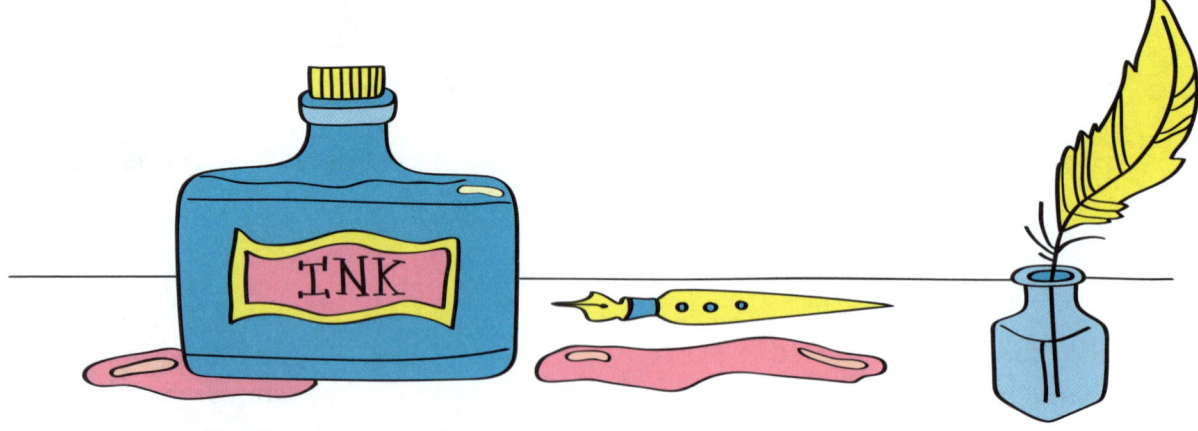

Answering Questions on a Poem

Now that you have read the poem a few times, you should find that you have a fairly good understanding of it. When you take the time to 'get to know' a poem in this way, you should find it easier to answer exam questions about it.

Information Retrieval Questions
You may get a question that asks you to recount a fact or something that happens in the poem. This is an information retrieval question. You will only get a few of these, as they are quite basic and straightforward.

Knowledge-Based Questions
Some questions will be specific and ask about a single word, phrase or **literary technique**. These are knowledge-based questions and require you to use the correct terms accurately and confidently. Always revise terms before an exam. You can use the glossary at the back of the book to do this.

'In Your Own Words' Questions
Questions will often ask you to explain / describe something from the poem 'in your own words'. These questions are designed to test your understanding, so you should avoid quoting from the text and paraphrase instead.

Personal Opinion Questions
Wider questions asking about themes and the meaning of the poem as a whole will often be based on opinion or inference, and require you to give a personal response, i.e. express what you think about something.

These personal opinion questions are the most challenging type of question and are usually worth the most marks.

There may not be a correct or incorrect answer – it could just be asking what you think. State your ideas clearly and back up each idea with relevant quotes from the text. Having a specific example to reinforce what you mean shows the examiner that you understand.

Questions that ask for you to 'comment on the effect' and give a personal response are higher level questions, set to challenge you. If you have spent enough time 'getting to know' the poem and its themes at the first stage of the process, you should be able to answer these questions confidently and efficiently.

Helpful Tip…
It is your personal response that makes your answer special and unlike anyone else's. That is why taking the time to annotate, understand and 'get to know' a poem really helps, as it will give you the confidence to put forward your own opinions.

Specific questions normally appear at the beginning of a question paper and carry fewer marks. Wider, inference questions, which may ask you to **analyse**, **evaluate** and offer your own opinion, tend to be at the end of a paper and carry more marks.

Example Questions and Answers

Question: Provide one example of contrast in this poem.   1 mark

Answer: An example of contrast is 'weep with laughter'.

Helpful Tip...
You are not asked to provide any further details, just one example. This is a one-mark question, so don't waste time and energy adding more than is required.

Question: What do you think 'far beyond your ken' means?   2 marks

Answer: I think that this means something that is beyond your understanding.

Helpful Tip...
The noun 'ken' means 'understanding' or 'knowledge'. If you don't know a word, try to make an educated guess using the context and words around it.

Question: What **rhyme** scheme does this poem use and what effect does it have?   4 marks

Answer: This poem has a recurring rhyme scheme: AABB, CCBB, DDBB. The rhyme scheme creates a reassuring, rhythmic effect in that the reader can predict what is coming next – the last two lines of each stanza return to the same sound. This reinforces the idea that books can always be relied upon to impart knowledge. They are as predictable and reliable as the rhyme scheme.

Helpful Tip...
The answer to this question has two parts. You have to be able to:
- recognise the rhyme scheme (knowledge)
- explain the effect it has on the poem as a whole (your opinion).

Helpful Tip...

To work out a poem's rhyme scheme, use letters to represent words that rhyme. The letter A represents the first group of rhymes, the letter B represents the second group, and so on. When presented with a rhyming poem, quickly work out the rhyme scheme and write the letters at the end of each line, perhaps in a different coloured pen, so you can recognise and refer to it easily.

Activity 3

Answer the following questions on 'Books' and then check your responses against the answers in Section 3 of this book. Don't forget to note the number of marks per question and make sure your answer corresponds with the marks available.

Q1. Find an example of **alliteration** in the poem. — 1 mark

Q2. The poet suggests that the reader 'can enter other people's heads'.
What technique is used here and what is its effect? — 3 marks

Q3. According to the final stanza, what effect can knowledge from books bring to readers and what does this suggest about the power of the written word? — 5 marks

'The Listeners' by Walter de la Mare

First Reading

The Listeners

'Is there anybody there?' said the Traveller,
Knocking on the moonlit door;
And his horse in the silence champed the grasses
Of the forest's ferny floor:
And a bird flew up out of the turret,
Above the Traveller's head:
And he smote upon the door again a second time;
'Is there anybody there?' he said.
But no one descended to the Traveller;
No head from the leaf-fringed sill
Leaned over and looked into his grey eyes,
Where he stood perplexed and still.
But only a host of phantom listeners
That dwelt in the lone house then
Stood listening in the quiet of the moonlight
To that voice from the world of men:
Stood thronging the faint moonbeams on the dark stair,
That goes down to the empty hall,
Hearkening in an air stirred and shaken
By the lonely Traveller's call.
And he felt in his heart their strangeness,
Their stillness answering his cry,
While his horse moved, cropping the dark turf,
'Neath the starred and leafy sky;
For he suddenly smote on the door, even
Louder, and lifted his head: –
'Tell them I came, and no one answered,
That I kept my word,' he said.
Never the least stir made the listeners,
Though every word he spake

> Fell echoing through the shadowiness of the still house
> From the one man left awake: 32
> Ay, they heard his foot upon the stirrup,
> And the sound of iron on stone, 34
> And how the silence surged softly backward,
> When the plunging hoofs were gone. 36
>
> by Walter de la Mare (1873–1956)

Activity 4

Write a short summary of what the poem is about.

Remember to think about the following questions:
- **What** is happening?
- **Who** is it happening to?
- **Why** is it happening?
- **How** is it happening?

Example Summary

Here is an example summary. Compare it to your own.

What is happening?
This is a **narrative poem** about a 'Traveller' who arrives at a house, only to find it empty. It is clear that he expects to be welcomed when he states,'"Tell them I came, and no one answered, | That I kept my word"', but he finds only 'phantom listeners' and a 'still house'.

Who is it happening to?
The main protagonist is 'the Traveller'. The narrator describes the Traveller's experience of arriving at the house, only to find no one ('them') at home. The 'listeners', supernatural characters, are a presence, but they are not seen by 'the Traveller'. However, he feels 'in his heart their strangeness', as does the reader – they both know they are there.

Why is it happening?
The poet is telling a story of expectation – 'the Traveller' expects to be welcomed – followed by disappointment, when he receives no answer despite numerous 'smotes' upon the door.

How is it happening?
The poet describes how 'the Traveller' arrives at the house, tries to raise the attention of the inhabitants and fails. He uses sensory **imagery** to create a supernatural presence, as well as a sense of loneliness and disappointment. The narrator writes in the third-person, describing what is taking place both outside the house and inside the house, the contrast of which serves to underpin 'the Traveller's' sense of abandonment – when he left, 'the silence surged softly' back. The Traveller is depicted as an intruder and not a welcome guest.

Second and Successive Readings

As you read the poem again, keep asking yourself:
- What is happening?
- What feelings can I sense?

As before, look for any patterns, contrasts and themes that appear throughout the poem. For example:

Patterns:
- rhyme scheme – the rhyming lines are 2 and 4, 6 and 8, 10 and 12, 14 and 16, and so on
- repetition:
  - of the question 'Is there anybody there?'
  - of the rhyme 'head' and 'said'
  - in the language of silence and loneliness: 'lone house', 'least stir', 'quiet of the moonlight'.

Contrasts:
- contrast of action between:
  - 'the Traveller', who is 'knocking on the moonlit door' and his horse, who silently 'champ[s] the grasses' and 'crop[s] the dark turf'
  - 'the Traveller' and 'the listeners', 'Their stillness answering his cry' – he speaks, they listen
- contrast of images between the 'phantom listeners' and 'world of men'.

Themes:
- the supernatural
- loneliness and disappointment
- mystery.

Remember to annotate the poem. This book is meant to be written in by you!

Helpful Tip...
When quoting from a poem, make sure you copy the text and punctuation exactly as it appears in the poem. Use:
- square brackets to show any minor additions / changes you make to help with the grammatical structure of a quotation, e.g. his horse silently 'champ[s] the grasses'
- a vertical bar (|) or solidus (/) to show where a quote runs on over two lines, e.g. 'leaf-fringed sill | Leaned over and looked into his grey eyes'
- an ellipsis to show the end of a line is omitted, e.g. 'But no one descended…'

Example Questions and Answers

Question: Comment on the opening line. 2 marks

Answer: The poem opens with the main character speaking and asking a question. Opening with **dialogue** makes the reader take note from the start. We are immediately hooked and want to know the answer to the question, 'Is there anybody there?' It creates a sense of expectation.

Helpful Tip...
This is an open question. 'Comment on' does not give you much direction. However, you can see that it is a two-mark question, so use this as your guide – the examiner will be looking for you to make two points.

Whilst the example answer refers to dialogue and the question, you could also comment on:
- who is speaking (the narrator) and who 'the Traveller' might be
- the setting – 'a moonlit door' – and how it creates a sense of atmosphere.

Question: How does the poet use the sounds of words to help you imagine what he is describing?
Provide an example to illustrate your answer.

4 marks

Answer: An example of how the sounds of words help the reader to imagine what the poet is describing can be found in the lines, 'leaf-fringed sill | Leaned over and looked into his grey eyes'. Here, both alliteration and **assonance** are used to make the image memorable. The 'leaf-fringed sill', suggests the house had been abandoned and ivy had started to grow across the windows, and there was no friendly welcome from a resident; no one 'leaned over and looked' to see who was at the door.

Helpful Tip...
Marks will be awarded for using a relevant quote, using correct and specific terminology that relates to sound (alliteration, assonance, etc.) and providing your own opinion.

Activity 5

Answer the following questions on 'The Listeners' and check your responses against the answers in Section 3 of this book. Don't forget to note the number of marks per question and make sure your answer corresponds with the marks available.

01. What **form** does the poem take? — 1 mark

02. Who do you think 'The Listeners' of the title are? — 1 mark

03. This poem is full of sensory imagery.
Provide two examples and discuss their effects. — 6 marks

Section 2: Assessment

Now that you have the framework that you need to read and 'get to know' a poem, you should be able to use it to analyse the following eight poems and answer the 11+ exam-style questions that accompany them.

There are no longer any guided examples, but example answers appear in Section 3 of this book along with helpful tips.

If you want to give yourself an added challenge, you can answer the questions under timed conditions. Each set of questions (not including the 'Challenge Question') can be used as a test paper and should be completed within 30 minutes.

Following on from each test, there is a 'Challenge Question'. This is a higher level question that in most cases requires a carefully considered personal response. No example answers are given for these extension activities as there are an unlimited number of possible responses. The purpose of these activities is to encourage you to really think in depth about the poems. Helpful tips and guidance are given to help get you started.

Test 1

Daffodils

I wandered lonely as a cloud
That floats on high o'er vales and hills,
When all at once I saw a crowd,
A host, of golden daffodils;
Beside the lake, beneath the trees,
Fluttering and dancing in the breeze.

Continuous as the stars that shine
And twinkle on the milky way,
They stretched in never-ending line
Along the margin of a bay:
Ten thousand saw I at a glance,
Tossing their heads in sprightly dance.

The waves beside them danced; but they
Out-did the sparkling waves in glee:
A poet could not but be gay,
In such a jocund company:
I gazed—and gazed—but little thought
What wealth the show to me had brought:

For oft, when on my couch I lie
In vacant or in pensive mood,
They flash upon that inward eye
Which is the bliss of solitude;
And then my heart with pleasure fills,
And dances with the daffodils.

by William Wordsworth
(1770–1850)

Q1. What technique has the poet used in the opening line and what effect does it have on the way you view the narrator? — 3 marks

Q2. The poem is written in the first person.
What effect does this have? — 3 marks

Q3. Wordsworth suggests that the daffodils are 'dancing'.
What technique is he using and what effect does it have? — 3 marks

Q4. Why are the daffodils compared to the Milky Way? — 2 marks

Q5. In your own words, explain the meaning of the following lines:
'I gazed—and gazed—but little thought | What wealth the show to me had brought'. — 4 marks

Q6. According to the final stanza, what effect does the memory of the daffodils have upon the speaker? What does this suggest about the power of nature? — 5 marks

Challenge Question
What do you like or dislike about this poem and why? — 10 marks

Helpful Tip...
You might look at this question and wonder where to start, but don't panic! The great thing about this type of question is that there is no wrong answer – you just have to back up what you write with relevant examples.

Keep the analysis framework from Section 1 in mind and think about your own feelings towards the poem. They will not be the same as anyone else's and that's OK.

This question is worth 10 marks so you are looking to pick around 4–5 relevant examples. Don't forget, you need to quote them and then write about them.

Do you like a particular image that the poet creates? Do you like the sound of the words as you read them? Does the poet make a point that you agree with? These are all things you can consider when responding.

Test 2

School Run

Sprinting, we cram into the car, panting with satchels,
a pile of marking, sports kits, cricket bats.
The boys belt safe but squabbling in the back
with shining morning faces, scabby knees,
cross-my-heart badges on blue-blazered breasts,
pockets of marbles, scribbles of prep.
We turn the corner carefully. On Thursdays
the old pair in the Ford Pop potter down to the pension queue.
Fridays is tuck, a sweet treat for the week's end.
There, I kiss them, check their partings, try to say
things to make them brave throughout the day,
wave, and move off. Through the town,
familiar unknown people walk to work. I follow the van.
Daily I see two waiting at the factory corner.
They pause to pick him up, this big child,
taller than her, with bland blank smiling face.
She does his buttons, winds his scarf. Time lies:
he is older, she younger, than her face declares.
I wait and watch. She waves and walks away,
her shoulders lighter for her short free day.
The shabby van moves off. I come behind.
The next stop loads a wheelchair and a girl,
lifted like a bride across the threshold.
Here I can pass them by and take my route
across the straight moor road to where I teach
the clever children of the clever rich.
The rear-view glass diminishes the van.
Guilty at fortune, I accelerate.

by Lindsay Staniforth (1951–)

Q1. What technique has the writer used in line 5 and what effect does it have?   2 marks

Q2. Who do you think the narrator is and what is her job?   3 marks

Q3. Look at lines 10–11. What do these lines suggest about the narrator's feelings towards the boys?   3 marks

Q4. Explain how the poet plays with words in line 9.   3 marks

Q5. Why is the girl being compared to a bride being lifted and what is the effect of this **simile**?   3 marks

Q6. 'Familiar unknown' is an example of which literary technique?   1 mark

Q7. Read the poem again. What do you think a main theme of this poem is and why?   5 marks

Challenge Question
Comment on any poetic techniques used in this poem.   8 marks

Helpful Tip…
To tackle this question, look through the poem and identify as many poetic techniques as you can, e.g. alliteration, metaphor, simile, contrast, repetition and **enjambment**. For poems with an obvious rhyme scheme, you could also comment on this.

This question is worth eight marks so, to be on the safe side, and time permitting, you should select four examples from the ones you have identified to quote and write in more detail about. Choose the ones that you feel most confident with. In writing about them, you should try to explain what effect each one has on the meaning of the poem or the message that the poet is trying to express.

Test 3

The Tyger

Tyger! Tyger! burning bright
In the forests of the night,									2
What immortal hand or eye
Could frame thy fearful symmetry?							4

In what distant deeps or skies
Burnt the fire of thine eyes?									6
On what wings dare he aspire?
What the hand dare seize the fire?							8

And what shoulder, & what art,
Could twist the sinews of thy heart?							10
And when thy heart began to beat,
What dread hand? & what dread feet?							12

What the hammer? what the chain?
In what furnace was thy brain?								14
What the anvil? what dread grasp
Dare its deadly terrors clasp?								16

When the stars threw down their spears,
And water'd heaven with their tears,							18
Did he smile his work to see?
Did he who made the Lamb make thee?							20

Tyger! Tyger! burning bright
In the forests of the night,									22
What immortal hand or eye
Dare frame thy fearful symmetry?							24

by William Blake
(1757–1827)

Q1. Comment on the rhyme and **rhythm** of this poem and explain their effects. 4 marks

Q2. Which word in the first stanza suggests that this is not going to be a poem about a benevolent tiger? 1 mark

Q3. In your own words, explain what is meant by the lines, 'And what shoulder, & what art, | Could twist the sinews of thy heart?' 3 marks

Q4. Why do you think the poet asks so many questions? What effect does this create? 4 marks

Q5. In the fourth stanza, the poet employs an extended metaphor. What is the tiger's creator compared to and what is the effect of this? 4 marks

Q6. 'What immortal hand or eye, | Could frame thy fearful symmetry?' is an example of a half rhyme as 'eye' and 'symmetry' do not fully rhyme. Why do you think the poet has decided to do this? 4 marks

Challenge Question
Select three images from this poem and comment on them. 8 marks

Helpful Tip...
You can pick any three images that you like, so choose wisely. The trick here is to choose the ones that you are most confident with and feel you can say the most about. If the poet uses a specific technique in expressing the image, such as simile, metaphor, **personification**, etc., make sure you identify this and use the correct terminology to describe it. This will impress the examiner and prove to him / her that you understand.

To gain high marks, you should always comment on the effect that the image has in relation to the poem's meaning.

Test 4

After Visting Hours

Like gulls they are still calling–
"I'll come again Tuesday. Our Dad
Sends his love." They diminish, are gone.
Their world has received them,

As our world confirms us. Their debris
Is tidied into vases, lockers, minds.
We become pulses; mouthpieces
Of thermometers and bowels.

The trolley's rattle dispatches
The last lover. Now we can relax
Into illness, and reliably abstracted
Nurses will straighten our sheets,

Reorganize our symptoms. Outside
Darkness descends like an eyelid.
It rains on our nearest and dearest
In car-parks, at bus-stops.

Now the bed-bound rehearse
Their repertoire of movements,
The dressing-gowned shuffles, clutching
Their glass bodies.

Now siren voices whisper
From headphones, and vagrant
Doctors appear, wreathed in stethoscopes
Like South Sea dancers.

All's well, all's quiet as the great
Ark noses her way into night,
Caulked, battened, blessed for her trip,
And behind, the gulls crying.

by U. A. Fanthorpe
(1929–2009)

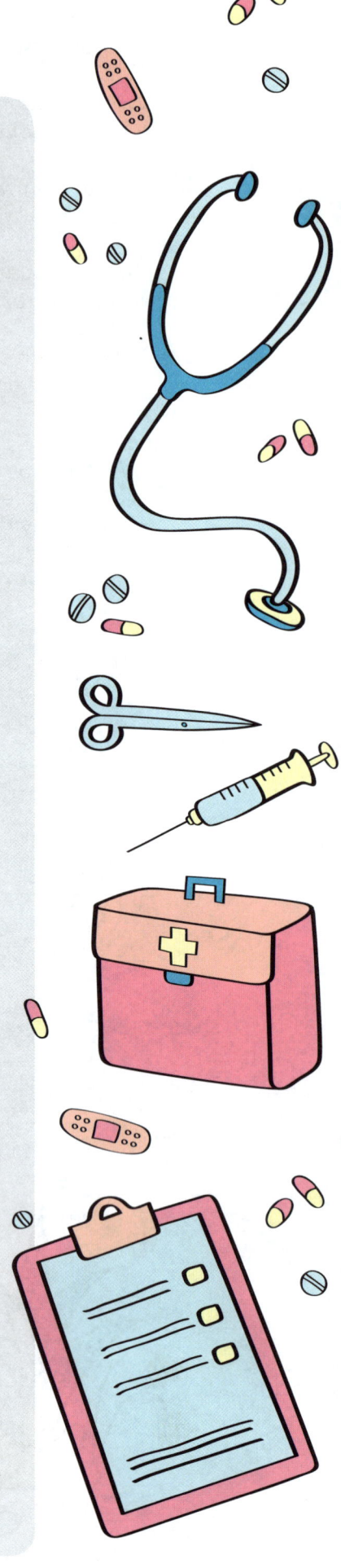

Q1. What does the word 'diminish' mean in the context of the first stanza? — 2 marks

Q2. Who are 'they' (lines 1 and 3) and what does the poet mean when she states that 'their world has received them'? — 3 marks

Q3. Who is the poet referring to as 'we' and what does she mean by the phrase 'our world'? — 2 marks

Q4. Find a simile in the poem and discuss its effects. — 4 marks

Q5. What do you think the phrase 'Now we can relax | Into illness' means? — 4 marks

Q6. What extended metaphor is developed in the fifth stanza and what effect does it create? Does it continue into any other parts of the poem? — 5 marks

Challenge Question
Choose one verse and comment on it. — 8 marks

Helpful Tip...
Where do you start with a question like this? You should read through the poem again and choose a verse that you like (or one that you don't like!) – as long as it has lots of things that you can write about.

Ask yourself the following questions to help you choose:
- Who is 'speaking' the verse, if anyone? (The poet, a character?)
- What is happening in the verse? Is anything happening or is it just description?
- Is there an image that I like? (And is it a metaphor, a simile, etc.?)
- Is the poet using any special techniques, e.g. alliteration, personification, **onomatopoeia**, etc.?
- Is there any direct speech in the verse?
- Where does the verse appear in the poem? (First verse, final verse, in the middle?)
- How does the verse fit into the poem as a whole?
- Why do you like it / dislike it?

Always remember to give a personal response for top marks!

Test 5

Not Yet My Mother

Yesterday I found a photo
of you at seventeen,
holding a horse and smiling,
not yet my mother.

The tight riding hat hid your hair,
and your legs were still the long shins of a boy's.
You held the horse by the halter,
your hand a fist under its huge jaw.

The blown trees were still in the background
and the sky was grained by the old film stock,
but what caught me was your face,
which was mine.

And I thought, just for a second, that you were me.
But then I saw the woman's jacket,
nipped at the waist, the ballooned jodhpurs,
and of course the date, scratched in the corner.

All of which told me again,
that this was you at seventeen, holding a horse
and smiling, not yet my mother,
although I was clearly already your child.

by Owen Sheers (1974–)

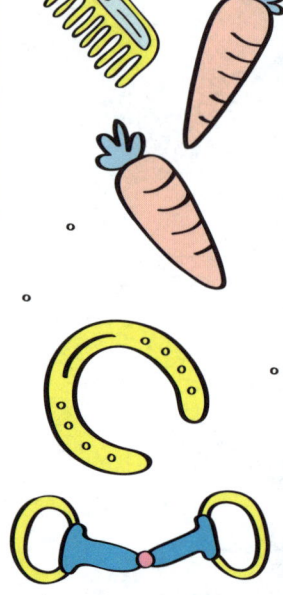

Q1.	Explain what this poem is about in your own words.	4 marks
Q2.	Identify two literary devices being used in the line, 'The tight riding hat hid your hair'.	2 marks
Q3.	Explain the effectiveness of the picture that the poet paints in lines 9–10.	4 marks
Q4.	What does the poet mean when he says, 'And I thought, just for a second, that you were me'?	3 marks
Q5.	There are many **lexical** references to horse riding. Provide some examples.	3 marks
Q6.	Why do you think the person in the photograph is 'smiling'?	4 marks

Challenge Question
Comment on this poem.   8 marks

Helpful Tip…

You are probably noticing by now that these challenge questions are open-ended and nearly always require you to make a choice about what to write about.

If you get a totally open question like this, don't be nervous! Use it as an opportunity to 'show off' your knowledge to the examiner and to provide your opinion. A potential school wants to get a feel for how and what you think, so this is the perfect way for you to show them.

With this question, you should go back to the analysis framework covered in Section 1 and use that to form your response.

Test 6

Summer Pudding

Someone else stretched for the cherries, under a warmer sky.
It must have dazzled as they reached the black-red fruit,   2
the size of eyes, out of the blinding leaves.
Now they wait, secret in white paper, for your harvest.   4

Stoop for strawberries. The shiny seeded postbox scarlet fruit
hides in bright bunches under brooding leaves.   6
Use two hands, one to push and seek among the green,
the other gathers, pulls. The ripe hearts pop, leaving the hull behind.   8
Heat hugs your bended back. Steal some:
they are warm with stored sun, and scented, heady.   10

Among the raspberry canes remember hide-and-seek and kisses.
Taller than you, they hang their best gems teasingly concealed.   12
Pull the berries; roll each with gentle fingers
To leave the white stalk bare. Inspect for insects.   14
Fill the glowing bowl. Inhale the spicy smell.

Hunker down for currants. Under the nets they hang   16
like Liberty print, pink pointillism, translucent spawn.
Pick with sharp nails each bunch. Fingers are sticky, stained.   18
The air is moist and fragrant, muffling sounds.
Thighs ache, sweat starts. Standing dazzles, dizzies.   20
Come to the cool kitchen and strip your spoils.

Now mix the pinks and scarlets with white sugar   22
until the juice draws. Pack into sweet bread caskets.
Freeze until February. When the winter threatens   24
never to end, thaw and turn out. Cap with snow-white cream.
One taste restores to you the day you made it.   26
Summer will come again.

by Lindsay Staniforth (1951–)

Q1. What types of fruit are used in the summer pudding that the poet describes and were they all picked by the narrator?   5 marks

Q2. Discuss the effect created in lines 5–6.   4 marks

Q3. What literary technique is used in line 9?   1 mark

Q4. Find a simile and discuss its effectiveness.   3 marks

Q5. What effect is created by the lines, 'When the winter threatens | never to end, thaw and turn out'?   3 marks

Q6. Explain the final stanza in your own words.   4 marks

Challenge Question
Using the poem as your guide, describe in your own words what needs to be done to make a summer pudding.   6 marks

Helpful Tip…
This is quite a quirky question, but an examiner could throw anything at you. The key to answering this question well is to make sure that you use your own words as far as possible, show attention to detail and relate the steps in the correct chronological order. Don't miss out anything important. (It might help to think about it as writing a recipe!)

Test 7

Success is Counted Sweetest

Success is counted sweetest
By those who ne'er succeed.　　　　2
To comprehend a nectar
Requires sorest need.　　　　4

Not one of all the purple Host
Who took the flag to-day　　　　6
Can tell the definition,
So clear, of victory!　　　　8

As he, defeated, dying,
On whose forbidden ear　　　　10
The distant strains of triumph
Burst agonized and clear!　　　　12

by Emily Dickinson (1830–1886)

Q1. Does this poem have a rhyme scheme and, if so, what is it? — 2 marks

Q2. In your own words, explain what you think the opening two lines mean. — 3 marks

Q3. What is the main theme of this poem?
Explain your answer as fully as you can. — 4 marks

Q4. What do you think the 'purple Host' could be referring to? — 3 marks

Q5. Sound is very important in this poem.
Comment on this with reference to the third stanza. — 4 marks

Q6. What is the **tone** of this poem?
Explain your answer as fully as you can. — 4 marks

Challenge Question

Do you agree with the argument the poet makes, that victory is only truly appreciated by those who do not attain it?
Explain your answer as fully as you can using relevant quotes from the poem. — 8 marks

Helpful Tip…

This question is looking for you to assess both sides of the argument and come to a conclusion. Your conclusion could argue for or against – it is up to you – but you must be able to clearly support your answer. The use of the word 'you' in the question casts no doubt that this requires a personal response.

Opening stanza from 'The Waste Land'

April is the cruellest month, breeding
Lilacs out of the dead land, mixing 2
Memory and desire, stirring
Dull roots with spring rain. 4
Winter kept us warm, covering
Earth in forgetful snow, feeding 6
A little life with dried tubers.
Summer surprised us, coming over the Starnbergersee 8
With a shower of rain; we stopped in the colonnade,
And went on in sunlight, into the Hofgarten, 10
And drank coffee, and talked for an hour.
Bin gar keine Russin, stamm' aus Litauen, echt deutsch. 12
And when we were children, staying at the archduke's,
My cousin's, he took me out on a sled, 14
And I was frightened. He said, Marie,
Marie, hold on tight. And down we went. 16
In the mountains, there you feel free.
I read, much of the night, and go south in the winter. 18

by T. S. Eliot (1888–1965)

Q1. a) Who is the speaker of this poem? — 1 mark
     b) Do you think the speaker is British?
        Give a reason for your answer. — 2 marks

Q2. What impression does the reader get of the speaker?
     Answer as fully as possible. — 4 marks

Q3. Find two examples of different literary techniques used in the
     extract and comment on their effectiveness. — 5 marks

Q4. a) Explain how 'winter kept us warm'. — 2 marks
     b) Is this idea surprising or expected?
        Explain as fully as possible. — 2 marks

Q5. What themes can you find in the extract? — 4 marks

Challenge Question

How do you think this poem might continue?
Write the next four lines using the first seven lines of the
given extract to help you. — 6 marks

Helpful Tip...

It is possible that a continuation exercise like this could be included in a comprehension paper. Whilst you might instantly see this as a creative writing exercise (which it is, partly), the question will help the examiner to ascertain how well you have understood the original poem, so it has a comprehension function. It will also give the examiner an insight into your creativity.

To answer this type of question well, make sure that you make links and references to the original poem. Maybe continue a theme or an image from the poem, for example.

This question is particularly helpful as it tells you to use the first seven lines to help you – but you could use this technique even if a question isn't as explicit as this. It makes sense to take inspiration from what is already there, but make sure you keep it original and don't copy directly!

Section 3: Example Answers and Guidance

The answers given in this section are examples only. For information retrieval and knowledge-based questions, your response does not have to be worded in exactly the same way, but it should address the same key points. For 'in your own words' and personal opinion questions, there are no correct or incorrect answers and your response may be quite different from the example given. This is absolutely fine – the important thing is to ensure that you have clearly stated each idea, provided a quote / evidence from the poem to back it up and then explained it fully.

Activity 3

Q1. Find an example of alliteration in the poem. — 1 mark

An example of alliteration in the poem is, 'motivates the martyr'.

Helpful Tip…
To answer this question you need to know what 'alliteration' is: the repetition of a letter or sound at the beginning of adjacent or closely connected words. It can be a consonant or vowel sound. Alliteration is often used to add character or emphasis to writing and can add an element of 'fun' too.

Q2. The poet suggests that the reader 'can enter other people's heads'. What technique is used here and what is its effect? — 3 marks

This is an example of metaphor. It provides the reader with a **figurative** image of being able to understand others' thoughts by getting inside their 'heads' and being able to 'read' their thoughts, as you would read a book. By using this comparison, the author is stressing the power of books.

Helpful Tip…
To answer this question, you need to know what a 'metaphor' is: a word or phrase applied to something in order to make a comparison, but which is not literally true. For example, 'Juliet is the sun', is an example of a metaphor. It compares Juliet to the sun by saying she is the sun. You know this can't be true. However, you can understand that Juliet shares many similarities with the sun – in the play *Romeo and Juliet*, Shakespeare portrays Juliet as a warm character, full of light and life-giving, just like the sun. A metaphor takes a concept that is understood clearly and uses it to help the reader better understand something more difficult. In this example, Shakespeare is explaining that Juliet is as warm and wonderful as the sun so that the reader / audience can understand Juliet's character more fully.

Q3. According to the final stanza, what effect can knowledge from books bring to readers and what does this suggest about the power of the written word?

5 marks

Knowledge from books can enable readers to understand more than their own experience has taught them. It provides an extended power of understanding. For example, if a girl wants 'to know the inner thoughts of men' or a man wants to understand a woman, they can read 'ink on paper' – in other words, a book – and 'enter other people's heads'. This implies that the written word can hold the answer to anything.

Helpful Tip…
You must focus on the final stanza, as this is what the question asks for, and include quotes to support your answer. This is a five-mark question, so it requires a comprehensive answer to show that you really understand.

Activity 5

Q1. What form does the poem take?

1 mark

This poem is a narrative poem.

Helpful Tip…
A narrative poem tells a story.

Q2. Who do you think 'The Listeners' of the title are?

1 mark

I think 'The Listeners' are ghosts who haunt the house.

Helpful Tip…
They are the 'phantom listeners' of line 13.

Remember, the answer above is an example only. You may have a different opinion. As long as your idea makes sense and is logical in the context of the poem, you should get the mark.

Q3. This poem is full of sensory imagery.
Provide two examples and discuss their effects.   6 marks

'And he smote upon the door again a second time', is an example of sensory imagery.

This image suggests that the Traveller is desperate to rouse someone. The verb 'smote' describes a powerful, violent action. It is one that we feel we can hear as well as see, as he is no longer merely 'knocking', but striking the door with force. The fact that we are told 'again a second time' implies greater desperation.

Another example of sensory imagery is: 'Hearkening in an air stirred and shaken | By the lonely Traveller's call.'

This image depicts the Traveller calling out, and his voice creating a movement or echo that is 'stirring' and 'shaking' the air – but to no avail. 'The Listeners' are just there, listening, 'hearkening', but choosing to ignore him rather than respond. Only the air is moving and reacting to his words.

Helpful Tip...
There are numerous examples of sensory imagery in the poem that could be chosen. The key to answering this question well is to write about the effect on the senses: sight, taste, touch (feel), smell and sound.

Test 1

Q1. What technique has the writer used in the opening line and what effect does it have upon the way you view the narrator?   3 marks

The writer uses a simile in the opening line. It provides an image of the narrator moving as though he were a cloud: floating softly and gently, being taken where the breeze blows him.

Helpful Tip...
You need to be able to identify the technique of simile and should then use your own words to explain the effect of the comparison – in this instance, the movement of a cloud. Remember, a simile uses 'as' or 'like' to make a comparison.

Q2. The poem is written in the first person.
What effect does this have?   3 marks

The effect of writing in the first person provides a sense of immediacy and a connection with the narrator. As readers, we are given the experience of being inside the writer's head, and feel we are looking at the daffodils with him.

Helpful Tip...

To answer this question well, you need to know the reasons why poets choose to write in the first person. Relate your answer to the poem to obtain full marks.

Q3. Wordsworth suggests that the daffodils are 'dancing.' What technique is he using and what effect does it have? 3 marks

Wordsworth has used personification. This technique helps us, the reader, to understand the movement of the daffodils by likening them to the human movement of dance. The image created is one of happy, expressive movement. It underpins the theme of happiness that runs throughout the poem. Normally, we dance when we are happy.

Helpful Tip...

Try to link the effect to the poem as a whole, as the final sentence in the example answer does.

Q4. Why are the daffodils compared to the Milky Way? 2 marks

I think that the daffodils are compared to the Milky Way to emphasise that there is a huge number of them dotted about and that their shape is star-like.

Helpful Tip...

It would be easy to just highlight one point here – make sure you include two separate points to gain those two marks.

Q5. In your own words, explain the meaning of the following lines: 'I gazed—and gazed—but little thought | What wealth the show to me had brought'. 4 marks

The poet is saying that even though he looked, and continued to look, at the flowers, he did not give much consideration at the time to the joy and happiness that viewing the daffodils gave him. He had to go away and think back on what he had seen before he could fully appreciate them. Nor did he anticipate the moments of pleasure that recalling the image of the daffodils would bring him in the future.

Helpful Tip...
When a question asks you to explain 'in your own words', it means that you must not use or repeat words from the poem, but 'translate' them into your own words to show that you understand their meaning.

Q6. According to the final stanza, what effect does the memory of the daffodils have upon the speaker? What does this suggest about the power of nature?

5 marks

It is a memory that often comes back to the poet when he is relaxing on 'his couch': 'they flash upon that inward eye'. When he has this vision it makes him happy as his 'heart with pleasure fills'. His heart is personified as it 'dances with the daffodils'. This suggests that nature has sights and experiences within it, which can make humans feel happy and content, and which they can always carry with them in their thoughts and memories.

Helpful Tip...
This is a five-mark question, the highest number of marks so far, and therefore needs adequate analysis and quotations. Focus on the final stanza as directed by the question. Don't forget to address both parts of the question.

Test 2

Q1. What technique has the writer used in line 5 and what effect does it have?

2 marks

The writer uses alliteration in line 5. It emphasises and reinforces the image of the children going to school in their smart uniforms, proudly displaying their school crest 'on their breasts'.

Helpful Tip...
In this question, you must identify the technique and explain the impact it has upon the meaning of the poem.

Q2. Who do you think the narrator is and what is her job?

3 marks

I think that the narrator is the boys' mother, as she kisses them and drops them off for school. I think she is a teacher because she refers to 'a pile of marking' and, at the end of the poem, says, '… I teach | the clever children of the clever rich'.

Helpful Tip...
Always use quotes to back up your answers.

Q3. Look at lines 10–11. What do these lines suggest about the narrator's feelings towards the boys? 3 marks

The poet is explaining how she feels about dropping the children off. She kisses them and checks 'their partings', ensuring that they look smart. She feels responsible for their appearance. She also cares and worries about them: she tries 'to say things to make them brave', which suggests she understands they might have a difficult day ahead or challenges to face. This shows her sense of responsibility for their well-being, as well as how they look.

Helpful Tip...
Try to find at least two points and back them up with quotes.

Q4. Explain how the poet plays with words in line 9. 3 marks

Rather than saying 'weekend', the poet has separated the words 'week' and 'end' to provide a different meaning. In a school week, the 'week's end' is the Friday, in preparation for the 'weekend'. The idea of a 'sweet treat for the week's end' implies a reward for the week's work and a warm welcome for a long-awaited weekend.

Helpful Tip...
A simple question, this holds three marks, so you must add enough content to make your answer solid. The key here is to realise that the poet is not talking about the weekend, but the last day of the school week. The final sentence is not necessary, but would show how well you understand the poem for a sophisticated response.

Q5. Why is the girl being compared to a bride being lifted and what is the effect of this simile? 3 marks

The girl is being compared to a bride being lifted 'across the threshold' because she is disabled and has to be lifted from her wheelchair into the van, using the same hold as a bridegroom. It provides a sad image, as a bride being lifted across a threshold is a symbol of hope, representing the start of a new life. We do not get this sense from the disabled girl – only that this happens to her on a regular basis ('daily') and never changes. There is no hope for her recovery.

Helpful Tip...
How you choose to discuss the effect of this simile is up to you and will be a very personal response. As long as you back up what you say with evidence and quotes from the poem, you should attain good marks.

Q6. 'Familiar unknown' is an example of which literary technique? 1 mark

This is an example of **oxymoron**.

Helpful Tip...
There is no need to write more as this is a one-mark question. Just because a short question like this comes after ones where you have had to think and write more, doesn't mean you need to write for the sake of it. The tempo of an exam paper can change!

Q7. Read the poem again. What do you think a main theme of this poem is and why? 5 marks

I think a main theme of this poem is gratitude for what you have and realising that not everyone is so lucky. For example, the scene of the family's busy, animated and carefree journey to school and the narrator waving them off is contrasted with the 'bland blank' submissive smile of the 'big child' and the situation of the disabled girl. It is summarised well in the final line where the poet says, 'Guilty at fortune, I accelerate', which suggests that she knows she is lucky and feels guilty for her good fortune – but ultimately, she is happy to accept it as she accelerates away and leaves the negative thoughts behind.

Helpful Tip...
This is an open question that does not give you much guidance. In addition, it is asking you what you think and, therefore, requires a personal response. There is no right or wrong answer. To score high marks, identify a theme that you understand and can write about confidently. Use two to three quotes to support your answer.

Test 3

Q1. Comment on the rhyme and rhythm of this poem and explain their effects.

4 marks

The rhyme scheme is regular and each verse is made up of rhyming couplets. The rhythm is also regular. Its hammering beat reinforces the image of the blacksmith in verse four. Both elements are simple and regular in structure, in keeping with the central idea of the poem: who created a creature like this?

Helpful Tip...

Remember the difference between rhyme and rhythm – they are two different things. Rhyme is the matching of sounds, most often at the end of lines in poetry. Rhythm is the pattern created by **stressing** certain words / **syllables** in a poem.

Reading a poem out loud will help you to hear and identify both its rhythm and rhyme more easily. Of course, you can't read out loud in the exam, but try to sound the poem out in your head. The more poetry you read aloud at home or in class, the easier it will be to do this in your head when needed. It is also helpful to listen to poems read by others – teachers, friends and as audio books.

Q2. Which word in the first stanza suggests that this is not going to be a poem about a benevolent tiger?

1 mark

The word 'fearful' suggests this.

Helpful Tip...

Sometimes a question will contain a tricky word like 'benevolent'. If you don't know the word, then you have to make a guess from the context. If you read on, you will get clues from words like 'dread' and 'deadly', which should allow you to make an educated guess that 'benevolent' has a meaning that contrasts with this.

Q3. In your own words, explain what is meant by the lines, 'And what shoulder, & what art, | Could twist the sinews of thy heart'.

3 marks

This phrase is asking what physical power and what craftsmanship can make a creature like this and bring it to life.

Helpful Tip...
Remember to use your own words and not any from the poem when directed to. Make your own translation. If it looks difficult at first, break the words and phrases down and tackle them individually or in small sections.

Q4. Why do you think the poet asks so many questions? What effect does this create? 4 marks

This poem is full of questions. It opens with the main question in the first verse – 'Tyger! Tyger! burning bright… Could frame thy fearful symmetry?' – and continues to ask further questions throughout the poem. It shows the poet's confusion, and we, as readers, are drawn into the same questioning mind-set. We start to think. Each verse addresses a different question. For instance, the second verse questions 'the fire' in the tiger's 'eyes', while the third verse asks how the tiger was finally created. The poem ends with the same question that it starts with, suggesting there is no answer. Both reader and poet remain frustrated, not knowing but still questioning.

Helpful Tip...
You need to have a good understanding of the poem to answer this question well and should make reference to it as a whole, using relevant quotes from different sections to demonstrate your knowledge and understanding. Normally, when questions are posed within a poem, it is to make the reader or poet – or both – think. Always consider whether the questions asked in a poem are answered by the end or not and then comment on this.

Q5. In the fourth stanza, the poet employs an extended metaphor. What is the tiger's creator compared to and what is the effect of this? 4 marks

In the fourth stanza, the poet compares the tiger's creator to a blacksmith, forging the animal in a 'furnace'. The poet uses the nouns 'hammer', 'chain' and 'anvil' to extend this image. I think that the use of extended metaphor serves to strengthen the image in the reader's mind, emphasising the labour and toil that has ultimately created a horrible 'deadly terror'.

Helpful Tip...
An extended metaphor is when a comparison is continued at length through multiple linked words, phrases and images. It is used to emphasise an image or point. By explaining how the extended metaphor works, you will show that you fully understand the concept. Marks will be given for understanding, a clear explanation of your opinion and the use of quotes.

Q6. 'What immortal hand or eye, | Could frame thy fearful symmetry?' is an example of a half rhyme as 'eye' and 'symmetry' do not fully rhyme. Why do you think the poet has decided to do this? **4 marks**

I think that the poet has decided to do this because he is asking a question that does not have a simple answer. Even at the end of the poem, he repeats it and asks the same question because it has still not been answered. The use of a half rhyme, with its imperfect rhyme sound, reinforces the conflict in the poem and the fact that the questions cannot be answered.

Helpful Tip...
To answer this question, you need to know what a half rhyme is and what effects it can produce. A half rhyme is a rhyme formed by words with similar but not identical sounds and often leaves a sense of not sounding quite right – this is sometimes called 'discordant'.

Test 4

Q1. What does the word 'diminish' mean in the context of the first stanza? **2 marks**

The word 'diminish' means 'to make less' or 'to reduce' and, in this case, means that the visitors are leaving.

Helpful Tip...
The best way to answer a question like this is to give a standard definition and then explain what it means in the poem specifically.

Q2. Who are 'they' (lines 1 and 3) and what does the poet mean when she states that 'their world has received them'? **3 marks**

'They' refers to the visitors coming to see the patients in the hospital. 'Their world has received them' suggests that the visitors have returned home, back to 'their world', and slipped back into their own lives easily – they have been 'received' seamlessly. It gives the impression they may forget those in hospital once they get back into their own 'world'.

Helpful Tip...
This is a three-mark question that requires a two-part explanation. The second part requires you to explain both a place and an action.

Q3. Who is the poet referring to as 'we' and what does she mean by the phrase 'our world'?   2 marks

'We' refers to the patients. Their 'world' is the world of the hospital, which is clinical, medicinal, and full of 'thermometers and bowels'.

Helpful Tip...
Whilst this is very similar to question one, this is only worth two marks. The definition of 'our world' is simpler and only requires an explanation of place.

Q4. Find a simile in the poem and discuss its effects.   1 mark

'Outside | Darkness descends like an eyelid' is an example of a simile. It likens the coming darkness outside to the closing of an eyelid, which suggests it is sudden and encompassing. When you shut your eyes, there is usually sudden and total darkness. It fits well with the poem's theme of people who are ill, sleeping. It further implies never waking, i.e. death, and that for some, it may never get light again.

Helpful Tip...
You need to identify a simile and explain what it means. This would get you two marks. To gain more marks, you must provide greater depth, making further links and relating it to a theme in the poem as a whole.

Q5. What do you think the phrase 'Now we can relax | Into illness' means?   4 marks

I think that this suggests the patients put on a show when they have visitors, trying to reassure friends and family that they aren't in pain and that things will be OK. But when the visitors go, they 'can relax | Into illness' – they can show their pain and fears in a relaxed way and not have to worry about hiding anything. They are together in the same situation, so they can do and say things that might be awkward or embarrassing in front of people who are fit and healthy – those from the 'other world'.

Helpful Tip...
This is asking your opinion – there is no definitive right or wrong answer. As long as you put forward your case well, and use quotes and logical argument to support your answer, you should receive good marks.

Q6. What extended metaphor is developed in the fifth stanza and what effect does it create? Does it continue into any other parts of the poem?

5 marks

The extended metaphor is one of performance, as though the patients are practising their moves. The words 'rehearse', 'repertoire', 'movements' and 'shuffles' all suggest a form of movement and dance. It is picked up again in the sixth stanza, when doctors are likened to 'South Sea dancers'. I think this metaphor creates a sense of routine and reliability but also a sense of camaraderie between those in the hospital (doctors and patients), as they are all part of the same show.

Helpful Tip...
This is three questions in one! The easiest parts to address are identifying the extended metaphor and finding further examples. This will guarantee you two to three marks. Other marks will be gained through thoughtful analysis of its effectiveness and a sophisticated personal response.

Test 5

Q1. Explain what this poem is about in your own words.

4 marks

I think this poem is about a boy finding an old photograph of his mother when she was seventeen. It shows her holding a horse and dressed in horse-riding gear. When he first looks at the picture, he almost thinks it's him because of the close family resemblance, but then he realises it can't be because of what she is wearing and the date, which is before he was born.

Helpful Tip...

This question is testing how well you understand the 'story' of the poem, i.e. what happens in it. If you always read a poem in the way described in Section 1 of this book, you should find this a relatively straightforward type of question to answer. The one thing that you need to remember is to use 'your own words'.

Q2. Identify two literary devices being used in the line, 'The tight riding hat hid your hair'. **2 marks**

Two literary devices being used are alliteration ('hat hid') and assonance ('tight riding').

Helpful Tip...

Assonance is the repetition of vowel sounds in nearby words.

Q3. Explain the effectiveness of the picture that the poet paints in lines 9–10. **4 marks**

This image is describing the background in the photograph and how the scene has been captured on film. 'The blown trees were still in the background' is an example of **paradox** – the trees are moving yet motionless at the same time because they have been captured by a camera. The phrase 'the sky was grained by old film stock' shows that the quality of the film was not good as it made markings ('grains') on the photograph. This description helps to reinforce the age of the photograph and the theme of nostalgia.

Helpful Tip...

In answering this question, you must look at both lines and try to comment on both. It is likely that you may not know what 'old film stock' (used in old-fashioned cameras, before digital) is, and you may have to make a guess. But if you think about the meaning of the word 'grained' and the adjective 'grainy', then you could make an educated guess as to its meaning. If you can relate the image to a central theme of the poem, you will gain higher marks.

Q4. What does the poet mean when he says, 'And I thought, just for a second, that you were me'?
3 marks

When looking at the photograph initially, the poet thinks he sees himself in his mother's young features and literally thinks that it is him, because they look so alike. But this is only momentary, 'just for second'. Then logic and reason take over and he realises that it can't be true.

Helpful Tip...
This question requires a straightforward explanation question, but as it does not specifically say that your answer has to be in your own words, you can include quotes.

Q5. There are many lexical references to horse riding. Provide some examples.
3 marks

'Riding hat', 'halter' and 'jodhpurs' are all words related to horse riding.

Helpful Tip...
'Lexical' means 'relating to the words or vocabulary', so this question is actually asking you to find words that relate to horse riding. You would need to find all three to pick up full marks.

Q6. Why do you think the person in the photograph is 'smiling'?
4 marks

I think she is smiling because she is taking part in an enjoyable activity and also the conventional thing to do is pose and smile when being photographed. On another level, she is quite young, 'seventeen', and this was a time when she was carefree and before she had family responsibilities (her son). Her greatest responsibility then was probably looking after her horse.

Helpful Tip...
This question takes some thinking about. On one level, it is quite simple – you smile in photos and smile when you are doing something you like. This would get you two marks. However, to get higher marks, you need to put yourself into the shoes of the poet, who, as an older person, sees his mother as being young at the age of seventeen – a time before the responsibility that goes with raising a family.

Test 6

Q1. What types of fruit are used in the summer pudding that the poet describes and were they all picked by the narrator?   5 marks

The fruit are: cherries, strawberries and raspberries. The cherries are the only ones not picked by the narrator, as 'Someone else stretched for the cherries, under a warmer sky.' This also implies they were picked in a different, warmer country.

Helpful Tip...
Three marks would be awarded for naming the fruit, while the other two marks are awarded for an explanation of whether the narrator picked them all.

Q2. Discuss the effect created in lines 5–6.   4 marks

These lines contain lots of alliteration: 'Stoop for strawberries', 'shiny seeded postbox scarlet' and 'bright branches under brooding'. The playfulness of the language makes berry-picking seem playful and fun. However, the poet's use of the adjective 'brooding' suggests a slightly sinister undercurrent, as though the leaves do not want to part with their precious fruit. 'Postbox scarlet' is a cultural reference, helping to locate the setting as the UK (as well as summer pudding being a typical British dish).

Helpful Tip...
You can choose how you respond to this question but, to be sure of gaining full marks, two to three points should be discussed and correct technical references (e.g. alliteration, adjective, etc.) should be used in your explanation.

Q3. What literary technique is used in line 9?   1 mark

Personification is being used in the phrase 'heat hugs'.

Helpful Tip...
It is always a good idea to reinforce your answer with an example.

Q4. Find a simile and discuss its effectiveness. **3 marks**

An example of a simile is: '…they hang | like Liberty print, pink pointillism, translucent spawn'.

This is a dense, three-part simile, likening the currants to an intricate Liberty fabric print, a painting technique and fish or frogs' eggs. All of these analogies are visually similar, reinforcing the image of the small, round and abundant fruit.

Helpful Tip…

This is a tricky simile to define, particularly if you do not know what 'Liberty print' refers to (intricate designs produced by the London department store), or what 'pointillism' is (the technique of painting with small dots of pure colour). However, identifying the simile (there is only one) and saying it is in three parts should secure some marks, and then you could concentrate on the word you're likely to know, 'spawn', and explain the image that this provides.

Q5. What effect is created by the lines, 'When the winter threatens | never to end, thaw and turn out'? **3 marks**

This is a clever phrase, containing contrast: the idea of a never-ending winter, yet being able to 'thaw' a summer pudding taken from the freezer. It makes you realise that you cannot control everything – nature, winter – but that you can have power over our own creations, such as the summer pudding, and your own happiness, as the narrator does by eating the pudding.

Helpful Tip…

Once again, you can respond to this in any way you like. 'Discuss' is a very open term. As always, make sure you back up your points with reasoned argument and references to the poem.

Q6. Explain the final stanza in your own words. **4 marks**

This is like a skeleton recipe. It explains that you should combine the berries with sugar and let it infuse before encasing in bread. Store in the freezer until the end of winter or start of spring, when it seems as if winter will go on forever. Then top it with cream before eating. This will help you to remember the summer when you picked the berries and restore your spirits, as you know summer will return.

Helpful Tip...
Explain what happens using your own words. Try to explain every step without missing anything out for full marks.

Test 7

Q1. Does this poem have a rhyme scheme and, if so, what is it? 2 marks

This poem has an ABCB scheme. The second and fourth lines in each stanza rhyme.

Helpful Tip...
This is a two-mark question, so if you just answered 'yes' and did not describe the rhyme scheme, you would only receive one mark.

Q2. In your own words, explain what you think the opening two lines mean. 3 marks

I think that the opening two lines show a contradiction and mean that accomplishment is most valued by those who do not achieve it.

Helpful Tip...
As with all 'in your own words' questions, avoid the words used in the text and find your own substitutes to demonstrate that you have understood the meaning.

Q3. What is the main theme of this poem? Explain your answer as fully as you can. 4 marks

I think that the main theme of this poem is summed up in the first two lines: that those who never enjoy success are those who yearn for it the most, as it is unknown to them. This theme is developed in the second half of the first stanza through the analogy of 'the nectar', which can be comprehended only by those of 'the sorest need'.

The development of the theme carries on throughout the rest of the poem. The winners of a battle cannot 'tell the definition, | So clear, of victory!' as the losers, who are 'defeated' and 'dying' and are 'agonized' at hearing the 'strains of triumph.' This poem provides us with a moral.

Helpful Tip...

This is a four-mark question, so it requires three to four relevant quotes and explanations. To provide a clear and flowing answer, running quotes work well, interspersed with your own written analysis.

Q4. What do you think the 'purple Host' could be referring to? 3 marks

I think that the 'purple Host' refers to the winners of the battle, as they are described as having 'took the flag to-day'. 'Purple' is a colour associated with royalty and rulers, which adds a further connotation, suggesting that victorious rulers do not truly realise the value of what they have achieved.

Helpful Tip...

You would get full marks by showing that you understood the phrase, however, by adding your own knowledge – in this case, the cultural connotations of the colour purple – you are adding relevant depth to your answer, which always impresses an examiner! But remember to keep additional knowledge relevant and on point – don't add it just for the sake of it.

Q5. Sound is very important in this poem.
Comment on this with reference to the third stanza. 4 marks

In the third stanza, there is repetition of 'd', 'b', 's' and 'z' sounds. The alliteration of 'defeated – dying' and 'distant' is the most obvious and powerful, but is subtly reinforced by the 'd' in the middle of 'forbidden'. The repetition of the long 's' and 'z' sounds in 'distant strains' and 'Burst agonized' seems to further draw out the pain. The poet's use of sound serves to emphasise the theme of the poem; that not having something increases your appreciation of what you lack and makes not having it even more painful.

Helpful Tip...

To successfully answer this question, you need to zoom in on certain sounds and unpick their relevance. Concentrate on a couple of words or short phrases that best support your argument.

Q6. What is the tone of this poem?
Explain your answer as fully as you can. 4 marks

The tone of this poem is relatively impersonal. The poet is reporting and interpreting what she believes to be a universal truth. She is making a comment on the nature of success and achievement. She refrains from expressing too much sympathy or compassion, although superlatives such as 'sweetest' and 'sorest' and the adverb 'agonized' express some emotion.

Helpful Tip...
Tone can be a tricky aspect to comment on and can be interpreted differently by individual readers. A good way to think of tone is to ask yourself: what is the poem's mood or atmosphere? How does it make me feel?

Test 8

Q1. **a)** Who is the speaker of this poem? 1 mark

The speaker of this poem is a lady called Marie.

Helpful Tip...
See lines 15–16: 'He said, Marie, / Marie…'

b) Do you think the speaker is British?
Give a reason for your answer. 2 marks

I don't think the speaker is British because line 12 is written in German (a foreign language) and there are references to the 'Starnbergersee' and the 'Hofgarten'.

Helpful Tip...
Any one of these three pieces of evidence would suffice, but to be on the safe side, provide at least two to guarantee the two marks.

Q2. What impression does the reader get of the speaker?
Answer as fully as possible. 4 marks

Through the speaker's reminiscence, we know she was 'frightened' of sledding, suggesting a delicate and easily unnerved disposition. However, we know that she likes being in the mountains, where she feels 'free', which suggests she values independence and nature. We know that she likes to socialise as she 'talked for over an hour' and 'drank coffee' in the Hofgarten, but we don't know with whom. We know that she is a lady and from the higher orders of society, as she is the cousin of the archduke.

Helpful Tip…

The above answer incorporates four impressions of the speaker, backed up with evidence from the poem. However, any three would suffice and would get you full marks if adequately backed up with quotes.

Q3. Find two examples of different literary techniques used in the extract and comment on their effectiveness. **5 marks**

'April is the cruellest month' is an example of personification. April is given the human characteristic of cruelty. This is an unexpected comparison, as April is in spring and we usually associate this season with goodness, renewal and growth.

'Winter kept us warm' is an example of a paradox – it is an unexpected combination and disconcerting image, since we usually think of winter making us cold. However, if we think about the snow covering and insulating the ground beneath, this apparent conflict of ideas is resolved and makes sense.

'Summer surprised us, coming over the Starnbergersee' is an example of alliteration, helping to reinforce the element of surprise.

'…mixing | Memory and desire…' is an example of enjambment, which enhances the natural rhythm of the narrator's speech and 'mixes' the dead land of the previous line with the 'memory and desire' of the next, run-on line.

Helpful Tip…

Here are four examples, two of which would suffice to gain you two marks. There are others in this extract, which have not been highlighted – have a go at finding them!

Q4. **a)** Explain how 'winter kept us warm'. **2 marks**

This is an unusual paradox – that winter should be warming – but when snow smothers the ground, the earth underneath can be insulated, which could be what is implied.

Helpful Tip...
Using correct technical language ('paradox') will give your answer precision and credibility.

b) Is this idea surprising or expected? Explain as fully as possible. 2 marks

This is a surprising image until you think it through and then realise that winter can in fact keep the ground warm and feed it with 'a little life'. After all, snow becomes water when it melts and water is the giver of life.

Helpful Tip...
You can argue this in any way you like, as long as you explain your reasoning carefully.

Q5. What themes can you find in the extract? Explain them as fully as possible. 4 marks

The themes of weather and the seasons run through this stanza, with reference to 'April', 'Winter', 'Summer', 'rain' (mentioned twice) and 'snow'. The stanza ends once again talking about 'winter', giving a sense of completion.

Re-growth and renewal is a further theme that springs from this, with lilacs breeding 'out of the dead land' and the 'forgetful snow, feeding | A little life...' This provides a sense of hope.

There is also the theme of memory and reminiscence, as Marie looks back on a time when she was a child, as well as remembering the seasons and more recent memories, such as drinking coffee while chatting with someone.

Helpful Tip...
The example answer provides three themes, but you should find and discuss at least two (for a four-mark question) from the passage and back them up with relevant quotes. If it were a six-mark question, it would be safer to find three themes to discuss.

Glossary of Key Terms

Alliteration – Repetition of the same sound at the start of words in a sequence, e.g. Peter Piper picked a peck of pickled peppers.

Antithesis – The use of contrasting / opposite ideas and words (e.g. bitter / sweet or hot / cold) to create a balanced effect, e.g. 'one small step for man, one giant leap for mankind'.

Assonance – Repetition of the same or similar vowel sounds, usually close together, e.g. Fred gets his head wet.

Analyse – To examine (something, e.g. a poem) methodically and in detail, in order to explain and interpret it, with a view to giving your own opinion.

Annotate – To add notes to (a text or poem), providing explanation and / or comment.

Ballad – A traditional narrative poem, usually in short stanzas.

Blank verse – Poetry written with unrhymed five-stress lines (iambic pentameter). This form is thought to be the closest to the rhythms of everyday speech.

Colloquial – Language associated with informal conversation.

Contrast – To compare two or more things, such as characters, settings, opinions, tones, etc. in order to showcase their differences.

Dialogue – A conversation / spoken interaction between two or more participants, also known as direct speech.

Emotion – A strong feeling deriving from one's circumstances, mood or relationships with others.

Enjambment – A line of verse that runs into the next line without a grammatical break, also known as a run-on line.

Evaluate – To make a judgement or to assess the worth of something.

Eye rhyme – When words visually appear to rhyme (e.g. the words are spelled similarly), but are, in fact, pronounced differently, e.g. blood / mood.

Figurative – When something is described using images, such as similes and metaphor – it is it not a literal description.

Form – The physical structure of the poem – the length of the lines, the rhythms, the system of rhymes and repetition, etc.

Free verse – Verse with no regular metre or line length.

Full rhyme – A rhyme where the recurring sounds are exactly matched.

Homily – A piece of writing on a moral or religious topic intended to teach people how to behave.

Imagery – Descriptive or figurative use of language that appeals to our senses and aims to produce a visual picture, to convey emotions or to suggest ideas.

Irony – When words are used to imply the opposite of what they usually mean; a (sometimes amusing) contrast between what is expected and what actually happens.

Juxtaposition – When two contrasting / opposite images or ideas are placed close together so that their differences are emphasised.

Lexical – Relating to the words a poet chooses to use.

Literary technique / device – A recognised device or technique that a writer uses to produce a special effect in their writing, e.g. metaphor, symbolism, alliteration, etc.

Metre – The pattern of stressed and unstressed syllables in a line of verse.

Monosyllabic – Having one syllable. (See 'Polysyllabic'.)

Narrative poem – A form of poetry that tells a story, often including the voices of a narrator and other characters.

Narrator – The person who is speaking in a poem (e.g. the poet or a character), especially a character who recounts the events in a narrative poem.

Octave – A group of eight lines of verse occurring as a stanza.

Onomatopoeia – Words that imitate sounds; a figure of speech in which the sounds reflect the sense.

Oxymoron – A phrase that combines two contradictory terms, e.g. 'bittersweet' or 'living death'.

Paradox – A statement that contains two or more ideas that seem to contradict each other.

Persona – The assumed / fictional 'voice' in a piece of writing.

Personification – To give human qualities to something that is not human, e.g. 'The trees were whispering.'

Polysyllabic – Having more than one syllable. (See 'Monosyllabic'.)

Protagonist – A leading character or one of the main characters in a play, film, novel or poem.

Quatrain – A four-line verse, rhymed or unrhymed; the most common of stanza forms.

Repetition – The emphasis of an idea through reiteration (reuse) of a word, phrase, clause or sound.

Rhyme – The echoing of word endings that sound alike for artistic effect or as part of the structure of the verse. It has the effect of intensifying the meaning and binding the lines together.

Rhythm – The sound pattern of stressed or unstressed syllables in language.

Sestet – A six-line verse, usually appearing as the final six lines of a traditional sonnet.

Sibilance – The recurrence of 's' and 'z' sounds, such as /s/, /sh/ and /z/, which produce a hissing sound.

Simile – A comparison between things, using 'like' or 'as'.

Sonnet – A 14-line verse form with a distinctive rhyme scheme.

Stanza – A group of lines (a verse) that form one of the parts into which a poem is divided.

Stress – The force, length and loudness at which a syllable is pronounced.

Syllable – A word or part of a word that can be said in a single beat. A syllable may be strong (stressed) or weak (un-stressed).

Synonym – A different word with the same or nearly the same meaning.

Theme – Underlying ideas or concepts at the heart of a poem.

Tone – A reflection of the poet's attitude towards his or her subject, created by the choice of words. For example, the tone may be serious or light-hearted, intimate or detached, formal or informal.

ACKNOWLEDGEMENTS

Developed by Letts Educational in partnership with Exam Papers Plus (www.exampapersplus.co.uk) to benefit from their combined curriculum knowledge and assessment expertise.

The authors and publisher are grateful to the copyright holders for permission to use quoted materials and images.

The publisher would like to thank Lindsay Staniforth for her kind permission to reproduce her poems 'Books', 'School Run' and 'Summer Pudding'.

'The Listeners' by Walter de la Mare, reproduced by permission of The Literary Trustees of Walter de la Mare and the Society of Authors as their Representative.

'After Visiting Hours' by U.A. Fanthorpe, reproduced by permission of Enitharmon (www.enitharmon.co.uk).

'Not Yet My Mother' from *The Blue Book* by Owen Sheers. Published by Poetry Wales Press Ltd, 2000. Copyright © Owen Sheers. Reproduced by permission of the author c/o Rogers, Coleridge & White Ltd., 20 Powis Mews, London W11 1JN.

The first 18 lines of 'The Waste Land' from *The Poems of T.S. Eliot* by T.S. Eliot, reproduced by permission of Faber and Faber Ltd.

Every effort has been made to trace copyright holders and obtain their permission for the use of copyright material. The author and publisher will gladly receive information enabling them to rectify any error or omission in subsequent editions. All facts are correct at time of going to press.

Published by Letts Educational
An imprint of HarperCollins*Publishers*
1 London Bridge Street
London SE1 9GF

ISBN: 978-1-84419-905-1

First published 2018

10 9 8 7 6 5 4 3 2 1

© HarperCollins*Publishers* Limited 2018

All rights reserved. No part of this publication may be reproduced, stored in a retrieval system, or transmitted, in any form or by any means, electronic, mechanical, photocopying, recording or otherwise, without the prior permission of Letts Educational.

British Library Cataloguing in Publication Data.

A CIP record of this book is available from the British Library.

Commissioning Editors: Michelle I'Anson and Alison James
Author: Louise Lang
Series Editor: Faisal Nasim, Exam Papers Plus
Editor and Project Manager: Rebecca Skinner
Cover Design: Sarah Duxbury
Inside Concept Design, Text Design and Layout: Fixate
Production: Natalia Rebow
Printed in Great Britain by Martins the Printers